Spark Your Fun-Schooling Adventure!

Just for Teen Girls

50 FUN

Creative Writing

PROMPTS

Estera Janisse Brown ~ Age 14

Published By Sarah Janisse Brown

& The Thinking Tree Publishing Company, LLC

WWW.FUNSCHOOLINGBOOKS.COM

She discovered an old diary,

written in 1922, when she opened the lock...

_____

_____

_____

_____

_____

_____

_____

_____

_____

_____

_____

_____

_____

_____

_____

_____

_____

_____

_____

_____

_____

_____

There it was, finally. Our island. Our very own island. It looked beautiful above the waves of fog, but there was still one question to be answered: Why had they sold it to us for only five dollars?

_____

_____

_____

_____

_____

_____

_____

_____

_____

_____

_____

_____

_____

_____

_____

_____

_____

_____

_____

_____

_____

Postcards and letters from Paris began to arrive in the mail.
Many were obviously over 50 years old...

_____
_____
_____
_____
_____
_____
_____
_____
_____
_____
_____
_____
_____
_____
_____
_____
_____
_____
_____
_____
_____
_____

Write ten words to describe yourself as a child.

Write ten words to describe yourself now.

How have you changed in the past ten years?

_____

_____

_____

_____

_____

_____

_____

_____

_____

_____

_____

_____

_____

_____

_____

_____

_____

_____

_____

_____

_____

_____

We were together at the top of the world when...

_____
_____
_____
_____
_____
_____
_____
_____
_____
_____
_____
_____
_____
_____
_____
_____
_____
_____
_____
_____
_____
_____
_____
_____

You come home to a note on your door saying

"You're in danger, leave this city, but don't tell anyone."

_____

_____

_____

_____

_____

_____

_____

_____

_____

_____

_____

_____

_____

_____

Imagine yourself in a different century.

Describe an average day in your life.

_____
_____
_____
_____
_____
_____
_____
_____
_____
_____
_____
_____
_____
_____
_____
_____
_____
_____
_____
_____
_____
_____
_____
_____
_____
_____

Make a list of five things you're afraid of happening to you.
Write a story in which one of them happens.

_____

_____

_____

_____

_____

_____

_____

_____

_____

_____

_____

_____

_____

_____

Your aunt went on vacation and left you in charge of her candy shop. You knew you had a lot to learn when...

_____
_____
_____
_____
_____
_____
_____
_____
_____
_____
_____
_____
_____
_____
_____
_____
_____
_____
_____
_____
_____
_____
_____

Write a short story about something that never happened...

This summer, anything is possible!

Make your summer bucket list!

_____
_____
_____
_____
_____
_____
_____
_____
_____
_____
_____
_____
_____
_____
_____
_____
_____
_____
_____
_____
_____
_____

You live in a neighborhood where nothing ever happens. Then one day you walked outside to see mud splashed everywhere, and a mysterious pair of boots beside the door. A stray dog comes running toward you, and then you spot a tired grey horse, grazing in the distance...

_____
_____
_____
_____
_____
_____
_____
_____
_____
_____
_____
_____
_____
_____
_____
_____
_____
_____
_____
_____

Write about two sisters who finally cleaned their room finding things they had never seen before, including someone else's diary, old necklaces and a wallet with an address in it.

_____
_____
_____
_____
_____
_____
_____
_____
_____
_____
_____
_____
_____
_____
_____
_____
_____
_____
_____
_____
_____

List five talents, abilities or skills you wish you had.

Write about your plans to learn something new.

_____
_____
_____
_____
_____
_____
_____
_____
_____
_____
_____
_____
_____
_____
_____
_____
_____
_____
_____
_____
_____
_____
_____

Write a short story about something that may have happened to your grandparents back in the 1950's.

_____

_____

_____

_____

_____

_____

_____

_____

_____

_____

_____

_____

_____

_____

_____

_____

_____

_____

_____

_____

_____

_____

_____

_____

_____

What are the most important things to you in your life?

What would your life be like if just one went missing?

_____
_____
_____
_____
_____
_____
_____
_____
_____
_____
_____
_____
_____
_____
_____
_____
_____
_____
_____
_____
_____
_____

A distant relative gives you one million dollars,
and a quest to touch the world with kindness...

_____
_____
_____
_____
_____
_____
_____
_____
_____
_____
_____
_____
_____
_____
_____
_____
_____
_____
_____
_____
_____
_____
_____

Step by step instructions for making your favorite sandwich.

First of all you must go to the store and buy bread,

or bake it yourself.

_____
_____
_____
_____
_____
_____
_____
_____
_____
_____
_____
_____
_____
_____
_____
_____
_____
_____
_____
_____
_____
_____

And you thought dragons didn't exist...

What is your favorite weather and why?

Imagine a whole month with no other kind of weather.

How would your life, and your community, be different?

_____
_____
_____
_____
_____
_____
_____
_____
_____
_____
_____
_____
_____
_____
_____
_____
_____
_____
_____
_____
_____
_____
_____

What is your favorite season and why?

List ten things that you enjoy doing in this season.

_____
_____
_____
_____
_____
_____
_____
_____
_____
_____
_____
_____
_____
_____
_____
_____
_____
_____
_____
_____
_____
_____

List five things that you would rather be doing right now.

It was the perfect morning. It was the perfect breakfast.
It was the perfect outfit. It was the perfect plan...

_____
_____
_____
_____
_____
_____
_____
_____
_____
_____
_____
_____
_____
_____
_____
_____
_____
_____
_____
_____
_____
_____
_____
_____
_____

What would it be like to live your dream?

Who would be part of it? Where would you be?

What would you do?

What would have to change to make your dream a reality?

_____
_____
_____
_____
_____
_____
_____
_____
_____
_____
_____
_____
_____
_____
_____
_____
_____
_____
_____
_____
_____

One day your parents announced that this summer was going to be different. Your dad handed you a backpack and said "Start packing..."

_____
_____
_____
_____
_____
_____
_____
_____
_____
_____
_____
_____
_____
_____
_____
_____
_____
_____
_____
_____
_____
_____
_____
_____

It was a warm day in early spring. You were planting trees with your best friend, when suddenly you both spotted something sparkling in the soil...

_____

_____

_____

_____

_____

_____

_____

_____

_____

_____

_____

_____

_____

_____

_____

_____

_____

_____

_____

_____

_____

_____

_____

"We're moving!" she said, "We are finally going to live that dream!" It was a dream your whole family once shared, but now all you could think of was...

_____
_____
_____
_____
_____
_____
_____
_____
_____
_____
_____
_____
_____
_____
_____
_____
_____
_____
_____
_____
_____
_____
_____
_____

A heart for adventure. A week with the cousins. $27.50 to spend. A bus ride to somewhere. And then the dare...

Write a short letter to your five-year-old self, and write a letter from your five year old self.

_____
_____
_____
_____
_____
_____
_____
_____
_____
_____

_____
_____
_____
_____
_____
_____
_____
_____
_____

What is one of your greatest strengths? Invent a character who doesn't have this strength. Create a situation in which having this strength is very important for your character.

_____
_____
_____
_____
_____
_____
_____
_____
_____
_____
_____
_____
_____
_____
_____
_____
_____
_____
_____
_____
_____
_____
_____

You live in one of those neighborhoods where nothing ever happens, and then one morning everyone on your street awoke to find small brown packages on their door steps...

_____
_____
_____
_____
_____
_____
_____
_____
_____
_____
_____
_____
_____
_____
_____
_____
_____
_____
_____
_____
_____
_____

It all began with a daydream...

_____
_____
_____
_____
_____
_____
_____
_____
_____
_____
_____
_____
_____
_____
_____
_____
_____
_____
_____
_____
_____

One morning you woke up to an empty house. You expected everyone to be at the breakfast table as usual. The back door was open and there was a note on the table.

_____
_____
_____
_____
_____
_____
_____
_____
_____
_____
_____
_____
_____
_____
_____
_____
_____
_____
_____
_____
_____
_____

Your character wakes up alone in a forest, with a kitten, a note and a backpack...

_____
_____
_____
_____
_____
_____
_____
_____
_____
_____
_____
_____
_____
_____
_____
_____
_____
_____
_____
_____
_____
_____

I always would tell my secrets to my dog,

but I wasn't expecting a reply...

_____

_____

_____

_____

_____

_____

_____

_____

_____

_____

_____

_____

_____

_____

The power went out, and stayed out for a whole month...

_____

_____

_____

_____

_____

_____

_____

_____

_____

_____

_____

_____

_____

_____

_____

_____

_____

_____

_____

_____

_____

_____

_____

What does it mean to be normal?

You and your cousins were spending the summer camping in the woods...

_____
_____
_____
_____
_____
_____
_____
_____
_____
_____
_____
_____
_____
_____
_____
_____
_____
_____
_____
_____
_____
_____
_____

Hannah's best friend had always dreamed of hiking the Appalachian Trail. It was all she ever talked about. Hannah is not the camping type, but she agreed to go, under one condition...

_____
_____
_____
_____
_____
_____
_____
_____
_____
_____
_____
_____
_____
_____
_____
_____
_____
_____
_____
_____

The road trip that didn't go as planned...

_____

_____

_____

_____

_____

_____

_____

_____

_____

_____

_____

_____

_____

_____

_____

_____

_____

_____

_____

_____

Change fifteen words in one of your favorite songs.

_____

_____

_____

_____

_____

_____

_____

_____

_____

_____

_____

_____

_____

_____

_____

_____

_____

_____

_____

_____

_____

She followed me home...

Everyone takes a risk at some point in their life.

Write about a time when you took a chance.

What was the result? What did you learn?

_____
_____
_____
_____
_____
_____
_____
_____
_____
_____
_____
_____
_____
_____
_____
_____
_____
_____
_____
_____
_____
_____

You sat on the rocks together as the tide rolled in. All the beauty of creation surrounded you. As the sun began to set you decided to stay just a little longer. When suddenly you realized...

_____

_____

_____

_____

_____

_____

_____

_____

_____

_____

_____

_____

_____

_____

_____

_____

_____

_____

_____

_____

_____

You were flying home from a mission trip with five new friends, when the pilot announced that there had just been terror attacks two other flights. All planes were to land immediately at their nearest airports. You found yourself in a city that you had never even heard of. The airline gave you 500 Euros each, and a hotel to stay in until the flights could be rescheduled...

_____
_____
_____
_____
_____
_____
_____
_____
_____
_____
_____
_____
_____
_____
_____
_____

From the time you were a small child your aunt told you stories about "Her Collection". She promised that when you were old enough it would be yours. You couldn't wait for the day, but were unsure about what she had been collecting. Then a box arrived in the mail. Confusion, curiosity and disappointment flooded your heart when you opened to box to find nine...

_____
_____
_____
_____
_____
_____
_____
_____
_____
_____
_____
_____
_____
_____
_____
_____
_____
_____

It all began as a fieldtrip to a historic light house ...

_____
_____
_____
_____
_____
_____
_____
_____
_____
_____
_____
_____
_____
_____
_____
_____
_____
_____
_____
_____
_____
_____
_____

"Take this with you" He said, as his wobbly hand inserted an actual roll of film into the old camera. "You are going to need this." She climbed onto the departing train, and waved good-bye from her window. He winked at her, and then she noticed that he was holding her Smart Phone in his wrinkled hand...

_____
_____
_____
_____
_____
_____
_____
_____
_____
_____
_____
_____
_____
_____
_____
_____
_____
_____
_____
_____

"Where do you want to go?" He asked. "Anywhere?" I replied.

"Well, missionaries are needed all over the world, is there a certain part of the world that has been on your heart?"

_____
_____
_____
_____
_____
_____
_____
_____
_____
_____
_____
_____
_____
_____
_____
_____
_____
_____
_____
_____

38253271R00057

Made in the USA
Middletown, DE
15 December 2016